D1308332

07/30/12

Cara Tadsen

Best wishes.

*Zakari Tata*

Zakari Tata

PARADOXES

ZAKARI TATA, M.D.

Printed in the United States of America
ISBN:1-4392-3648-8
EAN13: 9781439236482
Visit www.booksurge.com to order additional copies.

# Dedication

*Paradoxes* is dedicated to the good people who shoulder the world. These are people who give their lives and souls to enriching mankind and who are the moral conscience of society.

I also dedicate my book to people who are not afraid to give of themselves and who recognize the value of every individual; to the unsung heroes whom we turn to in times of distress; to the people we would call when we are allowed just one phone call.

I also dedicate *Paradoxes* to my father, Tata Askira, for his wisdom, scholarship, integrity, and kindness; to my mother, Laraba Askira, for her unique courage and vision; and to my sister Salma for being the most excellent model anyone could hope for.

I thank all the patients I have met and through whom I have learned to live. Thank you also to Cabrini Clinic in Detroit for opening my heart.

Finally, I thank the Great Creator for giving me the courage to stand up again in spite of myself.

# Acknowledgments

I am tremendously grateful to my best friend and life guide, Salma my sister, for giving me the confidence to write. I am deeply grateful to my mother for reading the manuscript every day for two years and for her encouragement. I thank my late father, who taught me to love books. To Angela Porter for being the first person to tell me I could write I say thank you for creating a new world. A special thank you to my American big sister Terea Harris for listening to every poem and to Brenda Gilbert for giving advice on life lessons. I would also like to thank Farouk Ali for editing the manuscript and listening to my earliest poems, and to Arletta Douglas for her tremendous support and editing. I want to thank Richard Turner for reading through the manuscript and for his thoughtful advice. A special thanks goes to Billy Cooper, who read the manuscript and who has been a very special partner at every stage of the book. I thank Saba Gebrai for listening to the poems and for moral support. An extra special thank you to Anthony Ambrogio for his editing. Thank you Michael Collins for your inspiration and editing. And to Deanna Bundy for being a living inspiration. A very special thank you to my American mother, Mavis Taylor-Hayes, Ph.D., who has encouraged me and provided invaluable technical assistance, kindness, and concern. Thank you Carolyn Gaddy for believing in me. And I thank my brother Abubakar, who, by turning adversity into love and success, opened my heart to see that the Creator gives favor to those who live a life of True Love. To Fatima, my sister for her patience and sincerity.

# Preface

This is a collection of philosophical poems that attempts to tackle life's challenges. Very often as a physician, I have to be a neutral and dispassionate guide to people whose values are different from mine. Or are they?

Values are a product of our individual histories. Human values are not genetically determined; for example, an Indian may have German values if all of his life was spent with Germans. The general human principles of fairness, justice, tolerance, and respect seem to penetrate our psyche early in life. These core principles transcend all culture systems. Other beliefs and behaviors are determined by our responses to different challenges. These responses depend on our unique perception of different life experiences and learned value systems.

Human moral difficulties often revolve around doing what we perceive is right, for what seems right today may be inappropriate tomorrow. At other times, what appears to be the right course of action may not be morally acceptable to others. Success often is based on good luck and the ability to adapt to changing circumstances that necessitate adjusting one's responses. As humans, we have the ability to respect different opinions, for we have all walked different paths. It is important that we seek to understand those whose values we do not share. To quote Kwame Appiah, paraphrasing Hegel, "tragedy does not result from the war between good and evil; tragedy results from the war between good and good." This struggle can be external (between humans) or internal (within the individual).

Mankind has been in search of the truth from creation. The truth is never easily defined because different situations present conditions where conventional wisdoms may be questioned. As we seek to grow, we have to exchange ideas with each other. Every human is a source of knowledge in the search for the truth. Many times before we decide on the substance of a message, we consider the value system of the proponent versus the substance of the message. The usual tendency is to agree with the message if the proponent is a member of our value system, and to be less inclined to agree if the proponent has a different value system. It is this paradoxical attitude to life that provides the inspiration for this book.

The following disclaimer is necessary because I am often asked if my poetry reflects my personal experiences. The only portions that apply to me personally are "My Father," "Dearest Mother," "To All My Nieces," and "My Friend Esther." The rest of these poems express emotions and experiences that others, whose lives have touched mine, have shared with me .

To Baba, this is your book, your love, your heart.

To Mama who still thinks I have not studied enough,
thank you for the pleasure of being your son.

# THE POET AS TEACHER, THE POET AS ARTIST: A COMPARATIVE PRELUDE

## By
## Ali A. Mazrui

Director, Institute of Global Cultural Studies
and
Albert Schweitzer Professor in the Humanities
Binghamton University
State University of New York at Binghamton, New York, USA

Albert Luthuli Professor-at-Large
University of Jos, Jos, Nigeria

Andrew D. White Professor-at-Large Emeritus
and Senior Scholar In Africana Studies
Cornell University, Ithaca, New York, USA

Written as a Foreword and Prelude to Zakari Tata's volume of poems entitled *Paradoxes* (2009-2010).

Didactic poetry went out of fashion in some periods of Western literary history – but has remained vibrant in African traditions of both written verse and oral literature. Zakari Tata has sought to strike a balance between the Muse as a moral teacher (an ethical role) and the Muse as a detached artistic observer (a focus on aesthetics). This is the underlying paradox of all Zakari Tata's other paradoxes.

Classical Swahili poetry sometimes used the didactic device of deathbed moral advice either from a dying parent to an offspring or from a dying spouse to the surviving loved one. The most famous deathbed moral advice in Swahili is *Utenzi wa Mwana Kupona* [Mwana Kupona (binti Msham), 1810-1860] which enunciates ethical principles and religious advice in the concluding hours of a dying woman.

Zakari Tata is a live medical doctor rather than a dying patient! He is also writing in the English language instead of an indigenous medium of literary composition. This meta-paradox does not detract from the power of Tata's verses and their compelling moral relevance.  His poem, *Drums of War* is fundamentally an anti-war sonnet:

> *Men of valor*
> *Spurts of blood*
> *Tears of terror*
> *Smell of sweat.*
>
> *Rush of fear*
> *Scent of death*
> *Acts of courage*
> *Deeds of horror.*
>
> *Clash, crack, and bang*
> *Blood and death*
> *Sweat and tears*
> *Victors and vanquished.*
>
> *This mother's hero ended another mother's dream.*

This poet gives warnings about the risks of both wealth and poverty, and challenges us with dilemmas as to whether <u>kindness</u> is a higher virtue than <u>truth</u>.

Shakespeare [1564-1616] put some of his most didactic precepts in the mouth of Polonius – words of wisdom from a character in <u>Hamlet</u> often portrayed as a fool.  The most famous of these precepts from an otherwise foolish tongue were the following:

> *Neither a borrower, nor a lender be;*
> *For loan oft loses both itself and friend,*
> *And borrowing dulls the edge of husbandry,*
> *This above all: to thine own self be true,*
> *And it must follow, as the night the day,*
> *Thou canst not then be false to any man.*
> **[Hamlet, Prince of Denmark]**

With memories of the 2010 earthquake in Haiti destined to be remembered for a long time, Zakari Tata puts a lot of emphasis on the virtue of <u>giving</u>.

> *Giving solace to the despaired*
> *And thus earned the right to receive*
> *Blessings when they fall,*

*And shelter when lost,*
*And nourishment when parched.*
*The love of others overcomes adversity*
*And feeds your soul with grace...*
*I have lived*
*I have given*
*I have loved*
*And God walked me home.*
   ***[I Have Given]***

In the history of English literature great virtues were sometimes attributed to the peasantry and villagers – as in the case of Oliver Goldsmith's, ***The Deserted Village*** in which Goldsmith [1730-1774] idealized rural life before the morally corroding Industrial Revolution.

And Alexander Pope [1688-1744] tried to recognize in the illiterate man many great virtues, in spite of being untutored:

*Unlearned, he knew no schoolman's subtle art,*
*No language, but the language of the heart.*
*By nature honest, by experience wise,*
*Healthy by temperance, and by exercise.*
   ***[Horace Imitated]***

Zakari Tata also manages to identify the existential link between knowledge and ignorance. He sees the pursuit of knowledge as being a consequence of restless ignorance. In Tata's own words:

*The most knowledgable amongst us*
*Are driven by the fuel of their own ignorance.*
   ***[Ignorance is Knowledge]***

People who are fundamentalist in their religion often refuse to pray for those who do not belong to their own beliefs. Tata urges us not only to respect the living across the religious divide, but also to pray for the dead across that same sacred divide:

*What to do when the non-believer dies*
*I am forbidden from offering a prayer.*
*Yet once in my life*
*When life was tough*
*When I was down*
*When I was beat*

*When I was hungry,*
*This non-believer*
*Lifted me up.*

*This non-believer*
*Acted like an angel of life*
*Walked with the grace of the blessed*
*And cradled me with love*
*Yet he did not openly profess the Truth.*
        **[Non-Believer Just Died]**

Tata's strongest self-criticism is when he turns himself into a Martian who visited Planet Earth to learn about human beings. The visitor was impressed by what he saw in Europe and Asia. And then he landed in Africa.

*I went further inland and saw disease.*
*Running water was a luxury,*
*Yet everybody had two cellphones.*
*I asked the Africans "What say you?"*

*They looked at me the green Martian*
*All the African wanted was a seat on my spaceship*
*"Not this time," I said "for in Mars we like ourselves.*
*We keep our fortunes to develop Mars only"...*

*I fled to Mars never to return*
*"Africans are strange" was my report.*
*For never in the solar system were there a people*
*Who gave away their souls on a platter of gold.*
        **[From Mars to Africa with Love]**

The Martian may have been too severe in his criticism of Africa. Before travelling to Planet Earth from Mars he should have consulted the great historians he visited on Jupiter on the Martian's way to Earth. The professors and priests on Jupiter could have briefed the Martian more fully about the history of the Atlantic slave trade and of European colonialism in Africa. Perhaps the Martian would have been less judgmental on Africa in the face of such mitigating historical circumstances.

# Table of Contents

# A Good Person

What defines a good person?
Is not about a selfish desire
And not about need
Neither is it about feelings
A good person is truth personified

Goodness is a reflection of honesty
And is not about personalities
You cannot profit from goodness
Since your gain denies the truth
And the truth belongs to no one

So my friend, are you good?
A person that does a nice act for you
Is kind to you but does not mean he is good
If you define goodness by your profit
Then maybe you love yourself too much

To be a good person
Act morally always
And state facts accurately regardless
Of your personal feelings
And without regards to loyalty

Humans love to love
But we love selectively
In an attempt to shield those we adore,
We allow our emotions to cloud reality
Love and goodness are not bed partners

Celebrate the success of others
Help a person you cannot trace
And give of your heart regardless of love
Learn to define a good person as
Someone who helps others who are not you

# Paradoxes

I am poor in the land of wealth
Yet I am the king in the country of the wretched

I am attractive in the land of the blind
Yet I am ugly in the country of beauty

I am generous in the land of mean
Yet I am the miser in the kingdom of kind

I am a saint in the land of the debauched
Yet I am a sinner in the country of prophets

I am smart in the land of fools
Yet I am silly in the country of wisdom

I am sober in the land of drunks
Yet I am intoxicated in the country of abstinence

I am loud in the land of the dumb
Yet I am unheard in the country of music

I am strong in the land of the weak
Yet I am meek in the country of courage

I am celebrated in the land of losers
Yet I am lost in the kingdom of winners

I am full in the land of the hungry
Yet I am starving in the country of abundance

I am the champion of my lifetime
Yet I am nothing in the kingdom of life

# The Tyranny of Freedom

Thinking drives reason
Reason begets enquiry
Enquiry delivers answers
Answers produce reflection

Then the restlessness starts
And soon the deep thinkers become
Rigid believers of their thoughts and
Renege on the freedom of mind that let them be

# Who Knows What You See?

There are those who are victims of knowledge
And there are those who are victims of the lack thereof

Some plainly cannot see the issues
While some can see yet do not understand

And we have those who see only what they set out to find
Together with those who cannot comprehend the knowledge they have

We have many whose minds are locked and the keys tossed into the sea
And those who simply have no recollection

There are others who are afraid to know the truth
And those who think they know it all

A large majority believe what they are taught
With no regard to the teacher's agenda

The teacher cannot see your soul
As you cannot see his

Make your way the way of searching
Do not follow another's truth blindly

Let your history be your own
And do not struggle for ideas you cannot fathom

Walk on your way and watch the thorns on your path
And do not live somebody else's dream

# Let Me Be

Let me be
For I am me

Let me be
I am the truth

Let me be
I seek no foes

Let me be
I strive for peace

Let me be
I am for real

Let me be
I desire no pain

Let me be
For I judge you not

Let me be
For I seek not tomorrow

Let me be
If you truly love
For to love me
Is to let me be
That I be free
That I be me

# What Is

What is life
If no purpose exists?

What is love
If you have it only for yourself?

What is wealth
If it is a currency of pain?

What is joy
If you cannot feel it?

What is pain
If you bear it alone?

What is friendship
If it brings envy?

What is pleasure
If it is short-lived?

What is faith
If you cannot find it?

What is desire
If you cannot control it?

What is kindness
If you abuse it?

What is humility
If you despise it?

What is happiness
If you cannot buy it?

What is the truth
If you cannot express it?

What is hope
If you destroy it?

What is honesty
If you shun it?

What is this life
If you have to leave it behind?

# Happy Any Day

Wish me a happy day
Whatever it is you celebrate

Wish me a happy day
For a good day is a blessing

Wish me a happy day
Even though our beliefs differ

Wish me a happy day
For happiness is a good thing

Wish me a happy day
For I am happy that you celebrate

Wish me a happy day
For your happiness is my happiness

Wish me a happy day
For it is better than a sad day

Wish me a happy day
Because happiness breeds harmony

Wish me a happy day
For happiness harms no one

Wish me a happy day
For it lightens my heart

Wish me a happy day
For it warms my soul

Wish me a happy day
Every day of my life

Wish me a happy day
For happiness leads to heaven

Wish me a happy day
On Christmas
On Kwanza
On Eid
On Diwalli
On Hanukkah

Wish me a happy day
On Your special day

Wish me a happy day
On every day of the year

Wish me a happy day
And give it any name you like

Wish me a happy day
For happiness breeds life

Wish me a happy day
For happiness radiates joy

Wish me a happy day
For happy people have no time to hate

Wish me a happy day
And I will give you love

# Purpose

I will offer you light
I will show you the way
I will open your eyes
I will give you life

This life is a search
The search is a struggle
For when we stop seeking
Then we live no more

Life is about something
Everything has a reason
Every fallen leaf has a story
To live well is to study life

There is a soul in all
Inanimate things have a purpose
To appreciate the complexities
Is to marvel at this life

How do you know what you see?
Why do you live only for earnings?
Earnings are the currency of living
Yet life is the wealth of the universe

To stay idle is to avoid life
Hard work with no mind is love's labor
Not to try is to await a fantasy
So at least dig your own grave

# The Angel in You

Every once in a while
You are touched by an Angel

This Angel comes with no warning
Yet this Angel is welcome

For this Angel appears at times of great need
Look back and remember many Angels

Remember this Angel is a sign
You are chosen to be blessed

Take this blessing to give glory
The Angel does not want your love

The Angel wants you to prosper
The Angel does not need your thanks

To thank your Angel
Try to be the Angel yourself

To be like the Angel
Touch someone else with love

To be the Angel of love
Help those who despise you

For the Angel that touched you
Did so without regard to your feelings

So to truly be an Angel
Give love to those who love you not

# Drums of War

Drums of war
March of thunder
Whiffs of smoke
Clash of steel

Men of valor
Spurts of blood
Tears of terror
Smell of sweat

Rush of fear
Scent of death
Acts of courage
Deeds of horror

Clash, crack, and bang
Blood and death
Sweat and tears
Victors and vanquished

This mother's hero
Ended another mother's dream
By fighting this battle
That was decided for him

There cannot be a hero
Without a battle
Since humans desire winners
Then onward drums of war

The end never changes, win or lose
There will be tears
There will be pain
We all leave this life in peace or at war

Lullaby of love
Scent of heaven
Orchestra of bliss
Music of peace

Kingdom of heaven
Is where we all go
Losers or winners
We will nest together finally

# My Father

Who encouraged me to read
Who taught me how to study
Who was all about excellence

He taught me about hard work
He taught me the dignity of sweat
And the value of honor

He taught me not to worship wealth
But to treasure knowledge
And to be kind with my heart

He taught me to achieve
He gave me wisdom and ability
He allowed me to live my dreams

He applauded my wins
And cushioned my falls
He held my hand

This is to my father
Who taught me how to die
For a death well deserved means a pure life

To my father for whom truth was everything
For whom honor was king
For whom wealth was a burden

This is dedicated to my father
For he was so good
That his passing was the birth of my life

# I Have Given

It is not a shame to receive help
You have to make it through today
It is important to live proudly
With a straight spine
And a clear gaze
The look of those
Who have lived a life
That allows them the privilege
To ask and receive in dignity
Because they first gave in darkness
Of their souls without seeing those they helped
And carried on their backs the weak
And led with their hands the lost
And forgave with their hearts the damned
And begged the Lord for the wicked
Giving solace to the despaired
And thus earned the right to receive
Blessings when they fall
And shelter when lost
And nourishment when parched
The love of others overcomes adversity
And feeds your soul with Grace
That sings your song of deliverance
That screams with joy and ecstasy that says
I have lived
I have given
I have loved
And God walked me home.

# Wars

With an AK 47
A love of freedom
To lift oppression
And liberate equality
I am a fighter

The end to all dreams
My heart is pure
Death I fear not
Sacrifice is my victory
Forward we go

We need to fight the rulers
Corrupt, abusive, exploitative
To free the peasants
From the selfish landowners
Freedom at all costs

The struggle intensifies
Widows are made
Orphans are born
Pain is the currency
Change is liberation

The war ends
Our struggle is over
We are captured
We are chained
We the terrorists

But victory was ours
We liberated the poor
We expelled the rulers
The natives can breathe at last
We the freedom fighters

The wind blows in all directions
The results unpredictable
All winds start with good intention
Good results come from calm winds
Disaster looms from rough winds

◐

# Ann Arbor Arts Festival

Full of pleasure
Lots of fun
Dancing in the streets
Happy happy people
Dancing around the block

The musicians from the Andes
The veiled Muslim women hawkers
The African craft traders
The Rastamen with locks
And the happy Jewish children

Oh what a delight
What a beautiful window
It is a time for love
A sight to behold
As we dance the night away

The culture of art
The festivity of fun
The celebration of life
The beauty of mankind
The key is love

The world is full of passion
Energy abounds in all directions
Harmony breeds joy
Togetherness denies prejudice
What a wonderful life

Oh Ann Arbor Festival
Why just a week
Why not a lifetime
Joy should be easy
Pleasure should be effortless

A festival of love
How life was meant to be
This should be our yesterdays
This should be our tomorrows
I choose to live a la festival

❧

# My Friend Esther

Thank you for being a good friend. You came first as a patient, but you became my best friend. You always had a smile and a kind word.

Every week until you were too ill, you left a kind message on my home telephone wishing me well. Listening to your kind voicemail late at night was always the highlight of the week. You were ill, but you were truly concerned that I was well.

Thank you for your smiles. Thank you for your pleasant demeanor. Thank you for teaching me about courage. Thank you for sharing your strength. Thank you for letting me into your life.

It was truly a pleasure to know you. I called you as often as I could to listen to your kind words. I was meant to be your physician, but you became my healer.

You healed my heart with your kind words. Speaking with you always uplifted me. You had such a positive attitude most of the time. You were gracious even when you hurt.

Thank you for the laughs we had. We had our own private conversations on the phone, especially on Thursday mornings. You made fun of yourself sliding off the wheelchair in a bus. You shared with me the joys of eating catfish down south and your favorite Greek restaurant. You called in great excitement to tell me about the electric blanket your lovely daughter gave you. You loved family. You called to tell me that they were all acting funny because you were sick. You just wanted them to stop looking so sad. You did not want them to worry so much. You cared for everybody else. You were simply the best. You truly enjoyed life. You taught us how to live. If I ever heard you worry, it was only about your family's pain. Your truly lucky family.

I know you are up there eating ice cream and catfish and laughing at us. You are laughing because you don't have to take my nasty syrup. I promise you, I only gave you the syrup out of love. I was just trying to make you fat. I am sorry we tricked you by hiding the syrup in your food.

We had fun together. You were my dear friend, my kindest patient, and my teacher.

∽

# Correct Gently

You are not faultless
And sometimes you will fall
For you are not the Truth
Even though you have many eyes

Kindness they say
Is better than being right
And being kind does not deny truth
Being kind allows the learner to profit

Being wrong is a matter of opinion
A blind man cannot see light
But may see your soul
While both your eyes are blind to the truth

So when you correct,
Be gentle with the ignorant
For their views are narrow
Yet the Creator let them be

# Do We Know Us

By the color of my heart
The depth of my soul
The path that I walk
The vision that I see
You shall not know me

From the ache of my longings
The gifts of my charity
The intention of my deeds
My cries, my joys, my pain
Then you can know me

From the sound of my words
The songs of my voice
The deeds that I do
The face that you see
You do not know me

I am the ocean
Blue, strong, deep and soothing
My thoughts are mine
Your thoughts are yours
But together we do not know us

# Friends Indeed

Friends that ask
Are friends indeed

Friends who covet
Are friends of flight

Friends ask not of you
Friends ask of your growth

Friends who beg
Love you for the bounty

Friends in need
Are not after your health

Friends who love
Want none of your gifts

Do not give to a friend
Give to a stranger in the path of the Lord

The Lord has asked that you give fairly
Those who deserve do not always ask

A human cannot satisfy desire
For we all need more

So give in the way of the Lord
And give with loving kindness

For the prayers of the truly needy
Will shine your path of paradise

Yet the prayers of friends who ask
Do not exist to ease your path to heaven

# Life and Death

That life is sweet
And death is sour
That living is good
And dying is negative
That is what we believe

Oh you who behold
Oh you who are here
Ask your forebears
And your ancestors
Did they not love this life?

They loved this life
They lived this life
They laughed, they cried
They rejoiced, they hurt
And then left this life

We inherit this life
That they left for us
We knew not where we came from
And know not where we are headed
Yet this life is precious

This is the life we know
A treasure to behold
We are so pleased to live
The privilege is ours
Never to be taken away

But others have gone
Centuries of people
From days of yore
They loved to live
But had to go

More have left this life than have it today
The end is final
Timing is of the essence
When the time comes
The sun is set

This clock of life
That we crave so much
That we selfishly guard
Like we have it all
My own life supreme

Those who left
May feel better
That they left this life
That we love so much
That we have to lose

# Gifts of Poverty, Gifts of Wealth

Poverty is not golden
Poverty is not virtue
Poverty promises not heaven
Poverty is a test
Of your love for the Giver

Wealth is not success
Wealth cannot bring yesterday
Wealth is not an honor
Wealth corrupts souls
And steals you from the Beloved

To choose poverty is wrong
To worship wealth is sinful
But none of us can truly say
That wealth was our effort
Or poverty was our making

For the great Love gives
And the great Lord takes
To remain humble is the key
For poverty is not a badge of honor
And wealth is not a sign of victory

If wealth is your gift
Then use it in the way of the truth
Wealth acquired justly can lead to greatness
Greatness used wisely may touch the souls of many
Wealth in the way of the Love is an arduous task

If poverty is your gift
Then you are free of distractions
For poverty of wealth is not poverty of love
Bitterness with poverty leads to faithlessness
Humility and love build castles in heaven

# Memories

Best parts of life
Are felt alone
We are alone
Thou art alone
Can we be us?

Memories are mine
Pleasures are mine
Life's best moments are mine
Do we share memories?
Do we share myself?

I often wonder
Can we create a memory?
Can we create a past?
Whose pasts are we?
Can we make the past mine?

# Mr. Nobody

Hey Mr. Nobody
Silk shirt and all
Fancy pants and shoes
Jerry curls all cute

Cool car to the hilt
Gold chains to the tilt
Sharp cologne to go
Finest suit in town

Hey Mr. Nobody
Full of flash
Empty of cash
Just to be cool today

Hey Mr. Nobody
Walk that springing walk
Hey Mr. Nobody
Ain't nobody fine like you

As you smell good
Talk good, feel good
And jive good
The girls come falling in

To be somebody
You start as nobody
To be nobody
Just ain't about nothing

Hey Mr. Nobody
Darling of the barber shop
King of the manicures
Friend of the beauty shop

Hey nobody guy
No money on your somebody
No credit to your name
Just looking good

Hey somebody daddy
Babies shooting from your hips
As you dance à la gigolo
Running from your kids

Hey nobody somebody
I know you are the man
You are running on empty
Fine don't pay the bills

# Pass Don't Mean Go

You see a path
Don't mean walk

You see an opening
Don't mean enter

You see a sanctuary
Don't mean hide

You see green
Don't mean safe

You see competition
Don't mean fight

You see danger
Don't mean run

You see hopelessness
Don't mean despair

You see illness
Don't mean death

You see riches
Don't mean steal

You see cheap
Don't mean buy

You see available
Don't mean "take"

You see a bridge
Don't mean cross

You see today
Don't mean forever

Temptation is borne out of greed
Opportunity is a desire to grow

Only history will tell if your choice was
Temptation or your choice was opportunity

# Pain

No pain that hurts can stay
No pain is welcome here
Let not pain be your guide
That pain not be the way

The pain that hurts is real
Pain that is yours alone
And pain that does not show
Is pain that touches your soul

Let not pain be the path
Let not pain be the darkness
Let not pain be the door
That sets us back again

Let us seek the painless route
The path that is true
The path that is real
The way that opens doors

To avoid pain is to wake up free
To awake free is to seek no pain
The painless way is the path
That lets love shine

# Prophetess of Love

Yes they look to her
As dreams drive her

Yes she inspires them
While she lives on a wish

Yes she shows them the way
Though she follows her heart

Yes she gives them light
While she sees only stars

Yes she is their nest
While she lives on the edge

Yes she is their guide
Yet faith is her shepherd

Yes she is their rock
And she walks with the Lord

# Seduction of Power

A wish for humility
A desire for humanity

The absence of avarice
The denial of temptation

To resist the seduction of power
To avoid the corruption of position

To be called a good man
Is not about a life of poverty

A good man has seen power
A good man slept with temptation

The best of us walked away free
The worst of us succumbed

Those who have not tasted power
Those who have not seen wealth

Then you have lived a life of poverty
For the coffers of the people did not touch you

Yet the claim to greatness is not yours
Greatness comes to achievers not moralists

Your greatness is not your poverty
Your greatness is not your wealth

The attainment of greatness
Is a virtue of a few

Greatness and wealth
Are enemies of war

A sense of history
A life well lived

Moral courage with a life of poverty
Is doing the best of one's situation

Poverty of mind, poverty of courage
Rarely produce a great man

To attain power is not a virtue
Power with selflessness writes history

# Queen of the World

You love to give
You love to love
You love to share
You love to heal
Your time is here

You feed the poor
You heal the sick
You empower the wealthy
You enlighten the scholars
You are the unknown

You are full of love
You are a true gift of God
To know you is to embrace love
To touch you is a blessing
You are the mysterious

You radiate beauty
Your smile is a charm
Good fortune is your crown
Your planet is the sun
Bright, efficient, and radiant

You are a select person
You understand everyone
You are not the judge
Instead you are a listener
Who strives to comprehend

I am glad to have met you
Though I will never know you
For you are mysterious
And you bear gifts of love
From your bottomless heart

# Set Your Heart Free

Let the skies open
So the rains fall
Let the clouds thunder
So the rainbows sparkle

Let the sun shine
So the brightness radiates
Let the pollen fall
So the roses bloom

Let the snow fall
So the reindeer sing
Let the moon appear
So the stars twinkle

Let tomorrow be
So your heart can fly
Let the love be
That sets your soul free

# To All My Nieces

So much worth living for
You are beautiful, polite, and quite brilliant
You are respectful, responsible, and pleasant
You are full of kindness, happiness, and joy

Every day as I toil and sweat
I think about my wonderful nieces
I have to make your lives pleasant
I want to give you the best of this world

Do not thank me
I need to thank you
I am truly blessed
To have such wonderful girls in my life

I am proud of each one of you
You make it easy for me every day
For I know however tough it gets
I have my most loving nieces to hold my hands

Thank you for all you share
Thank you for the pleasures you give
Thank you for making our lives easy
For you have all been good girls

We have no tears from you
We have no worry from you
For you are sources of pleasure
For you are joy to all

# She Clings

She wants just one week
Lord grant her this
And you Lord know best

She struggles
She cries
She hurts

She wants to live
Death is not welcome
But you Lord know best

Lord of the Heavens
We are at your pleasure
You bring us and take us away

Thank you Lord
For this life
That I saw your majesty

Thank you Lord
That I saw your light
That you came to her

Thank you Lord
You were there in her eyes
As she struggled to live

# Cry of the Trapped Soul

You may take my land
You may steal my home
You may acquire my possessions
But not my soul

You may chase me
You may trap me
You may encircle me
My essence is mine alone

You may squeeze me
You may freeze me
You may squash me
I keep my spirit

You may talk to me
You may sing to me
You may cajole me
My thoughts are mine

I may shed tears
I may recant
I may follow your path
My life is still mine

You are the victor
You are supreme
You have conquered me today
Yet I am still me

# Dearest Mother

Dearest Mother
I lived with love
And left with peace
My life was pleasure
My life was joy
My mother was the dream

Dear Mum
I  knew love
I never wanted
I never despaired
I never desired
My mum the love

Mama
I was never worried
I was never afraid
I was never alone
I had your presence
My mama forever

Dearest Mummy
As I go to heaven
I will be at home
You were heaven
You gave me love

My Mother
You have my smiles
My prayers
My love
My heart
Will carry you through

To she who is love
I have so much work up here
We have to make it ready for you
You are deserving of so much
The house of love takes time to build

ᖗᖕ

# Depressed

I wake up with tears
And rise with pain
Yet I walk on
To see what today holds
To pray for tomorrow's visit

Yet I despair
The joys of today are not mine
Pleasure I know not
Tears are my comfort
Sorrow is my partner

I live a life to be desired
And have all that life can give
My presence is a joy to the world
Yet sorrow drags me on
And darkness is my comfort

I pray that I can taste
This life that others see
I pray that I can laugh
And share the happiness that abounds
That I feel hope and not despair

Grant me peace
For my burden is great
I continue to give joy to others
Yet all I see are storm clouds
While I await at Your pleasure

# False Tomorrows

Neither you nor I will determine tomorrow
It will be and it will end
It goes with the sunset
The twilights are our deeds
Tomorrows are wonderful if we live the truth

Avoid false gods
Gods of wealth
Gods of greed
Gods of flesh
Gods of "me"

The fools are envy, desire, greed, and competition
Against envy be supportive
To defeat desire love this life
Against greed develop contentment
In competition adopt partnerships

That is all that we can do
Life is but a short sweet journey
Every day is an opportunity
So celebrate the dawn of tomorrow
And you search for truth with the depth of your soul

# Fear Nothing

Have no fear
Fear no evil
For surely no evil can touch you

Did you not open your heart?
Did you not bless the Creator?
And give glory to the One?

Then fear not
For evil shall not touch you
And you do not know darkness

In darkness you see light
Your heart shines with brightness
Your soul sings with the angels

Then fear not
For you shall walk strong
And your path is chosen

No evil knows you
For you fight evil
And the forces of darkness are your enemy

Allow not fear to win
For your heart is clean
And you celebrate the success of others

Did you not praise the Most High
Did His blessings not touch you?
Did you not receive of His blessings?

Then you shall walk free
For your vision is peace
And you search for truth with the depth of your soul

෧෨

# Foolish Wisdom

If your enemy said you were a fool
You blamed your enemy for envy
You blamed your enemy for ignorance
Whether you truly were a fool
Still remains to be answered

For your enemy may have spoken the truth
For the truth is true regardless of the source
Truth hurts for the true path is difficult
Truth is the courage to accept your imperfection
Accepting the truth opens up doors of contentment

Your loved ones may deny you the truth
For they would have to share with you
The pain of acceptance
They seek you no pain
And so they avoid the truth

The enemy wants you to hurt
And so he pleasures in sharing bitter truths
True wisdom lies in separating
Your enemy's bile from the truth
Give thanks to your enemy for wise counsel

Let your path be of seeking truth
Open your heart to see the right way
For when you hear and act the truth
Then the enemy whose goal is to hurt
Now takes your place as the fool

# Miserable Man

I have been cursed, I have been banished
Thrown away to the wolves to tear at my soul
Thrown to the dogs to eat at my heart
I am the very scourge of good things

Where there should be happiness I see darkness
Where hope abounds I bring clouds
I who shut the door on pleasure
I who was cursed by the joyless witch

Why me? I who never harmed a fly
I who live for others, I who always give
Why curse me that I bring misery to others
Why make me the unpredictable paradox?

I am not deserving of anything good
My life is a dream yet tears flow in my veins
I owned the world but the rocks got me first
I drink scalding water in place of nectar

Oh my curser, my bad-deed carrier
Save me from grief, let me grieve alone
Do not let the world share my soul
I chose happiness but the painful hand got me

# Mistakes

A good person
A wonderful person
An excellent person
Made a mistake today
—Does not make him bad

A negative person
A dark soul
A person to forget
Did something good today
—Does not make him good

Any soul is capable of any action
As you judge the action
Do not forget the doer
For the evil may do a good deed
And the blessed may perform bad acts

A person not known for goodness
May respond to grace
He is still capable of good acts
Good actions should be rewarded
Irrespective of the doer

But don't let a few acts blind you
Actions may not always reflect essence
Think always with your head
Kind souls might conceal their good actions
While bad souls can hide behind a few good deeds

Have the kindness in your heart to acknowledge failings
You are just human
To err is to have tried
Failure is opportunity for growth
Failing is a bump along the path to perfection

# Mr Truth

The truth will set who free?
The truth will lift some up
The truth will smile on some
The truth will save some times
But for whom does the truth ring?

Who wants Mr. Truth?
Who wants to be set free
Mr Truth comes with goodness
Mr Truth comes with light
Yet he is not welcome

Yes we call Mr. Truth
We seek him when he is on our side
But we forget him when we need him not
We want him with us when we are right
Yet we hide him when we do wrong

You Mr. Truth
We crave you
We request you
We beseech you
Yet we cannot handle you

Say Mr. Truth
Where are you hiding?
Hiding in closets, hiding in hearts
Say Mr. Truth
You are so hard to find

You justify all human deeds
The just, the unjust, and the grey zones
You have so many colors
And you appear in many opposing pictures
And we take parts of you we need

Say sir Mr. Truth
You defy description
You are reinvented every day
You are reborn every hour every second
Mr Truth you are so controlling

Do you know Mr. Truth?
Do you really want him?
We speak of him
We call his name
Yet we run from him

Fly away Mr. Truth
Over the mountains over the skies
Fly to the moon
With all your might
Till you come back single and perfect

# Mother's Pride

Yes I am a mother
Beautiful and strong
Full of passion
With glowing pride

I am a mother
Full of hope
Desiring of life's bounties
For the products of my womb

Yes I am a mother
Shielding and nurturing
Protecting the offspring
That came from my loins

Yes I am a woman
Strong as the winds
Firm as a rock
Who protects this child

Yes I am mother
My child I will always love
That baby has my heart
True love unbroken

# Passing Through

I die alone today sad
My dreams withered
No American dream
No bosom friends
Just me, my bones and my soul

Friends of fancy
Compatriots of the night
Even as I take my last breaths
Friends of yore still promise
"I will be there to see you"

Yet I judge them not
For life is seductive
When you have strength
You want the material comforts
Who really desires the dying friend?

Well I desire life
And I desire strength
I want no car, no castles
No designers, no customs
Just to be me

It is okay to want
It is okay to covet
But as you go through life
Look for friends who will be there
Through tears and through joy

At times of trouble
Those who only laughed with you
Will not be around
For this is no laughing matter
So they have no place

Always enjoy today
But with the best of people
Who have your heart
Who will wash your soul
And who pleasure in your presence, regardless

# Non-Believer Just Died

What to do when the non-believer dies
I am forbidden from offering a  prayer
Yet once in my life
When life was tough
When I was down
When I was beat
When I was hungry
This non-believer,
Lifted me up

This non-believer
Acted like the angel of life
Walked with the grace of the blessed
And cradled me with love
Yet he did not openly profess the Truth

But the Lord in his wisdom knows best
This non-believer with the heart of charity
With strides of the walk of the chosen
Is not among the crowd at mass
Neither with the believers at dawn

Only the Creator knows
That he lifted me when the believers left
And he nourished me so I could praise the Beloved
Yet he was lost in darkness
And the Lord knows my heart

When this non-believer departs
My soul cries for him
For the hand of the Lord
Let him touch me
And I pray everyday
That the Creator shows him peace

Those who wear robes of faith
And who are mindful of their Lord
May the Almighty continue to guide them
That their hearts glow with brightness
And their insides are not in battle
With their outer cloaks of honor

The Lord knows best
The truth in your heart
And only the Love knows
If your suit is that of Grace
And if your soul is among the blessed

So judge not the non-believer who just left
And look for the non-believer in yourself
Let the exit of the non-believer
Be a reminder to you
That your best faith has just begun again

# Desire

Desire yesterday
Consummation today
Rejection tomorrow

Wait 'til you have
Tasted the true desire
It is permanent

You cannot consume it
It is all encompassing
It is beyond rejection

# Light of My Life

Thank you for lighting a fire in me
Thank you for allowing my spirit to soar
Thank you for the peace that you give me

It is not your pristine beauty
It is not your beautiful face
It is not your soothing presence
It is not your dimples of joy

It is your heart
It is your soul
It is your essence
It is your purity

I cannot describe how I feel
I feel calmness
I feel no need to own you
It is enough to have felt your heart

It is healing to have one day with you
One day with you is enough
For one lifetime

There is a peace about you
There lies an aura about you
That allows me to say
That the lava of Eden glows in your eyes

You are beyond a temptation
Dreams could not conjure you
Because dreams wake up
While you are real

You inspire desire for an endless life
While you still remind us of mortality
You are definitely worth this life

Somewhere somehow
I knew my heart was longing
The True one was somewhere

I could not describe who she was
My toes, my bones, my hands,
My spine, my nose
Would tell me when she came

She has come
She is possible
I met you
You touched my soul

&

# Perfecta – Angel of Joy

By the kindness of your soul
And the humility of your countenance
By the deeds that you do
And the learning that you share
May paradise take you

By the paths that you open
And the brightness that you radiate
By the minds that you grow
And the lives that you transform
May the prophets cradle you

By the grounds that you walk
And the footprints that you leave
By the tears that you dry
And the joy that pours forth
May your home in Eden be scented with roses and jasmine

By the hands that you write with
And the hearts that you nourish
By the directions that you steer
And your ageless wisdoms
May the birds of paradise serenade you

By the clarity of your purpose
And the convictions that you share
By the nobleness of your deeds
And the peace that you create
May the heavens rejoice you

By the blessings that you bear
And the gifts of your presence
By the purity of your heart
And the missions that you serve
You are a glory to behold

That you are the chosen one is clear
To behold you is an opportunity
To see the love of the creator
You come as proof of his bounty
That we may learn from you and drink of your fountain

# The Life of a Wanderer

Along the path
Out of nowhere
Following my dreams
Dreaming my dreams

Grasping on realization
Fulfilling, achieving, creating
Undoing, building
I came

I reached out to grasp the sun
While I acquired the world
I reached out to behold the moon
As the universe became mine

I shall make this life my egg
Fragile and delicate, protecting life
When I crack,
Behold, a new dawn

This path I walk
Shall shine for others
Looks very easy
But is laden with pain

To behold this life
To banish fear
And dare to change
The supposed purity of purpose

I acknowledge this life
I sacrifice pleasures
As I learn to walk
My dream that I dared to live

❧

# The Path

The path is right that has no end
The path is right that has bumps
The endless path is the path of Truth.

Truth is a search
Knowledge is all encompassing
Knowledge is limitless

The end of all knowledge
Is to say "I know"
For the best of us are seekers

If you have come to a conclusion
You did not seek,
The truth is beyond you

# Thank Your Maker

Thank Your Maker
That you are here today
You have access to transport

Thank Your Maker
That you can read this
You have eyes

Thank Your Maker
That you have co-pays
You have health insurance

Thank Your Maker
That you feel pain
You still have feeling

Thank Your Maker
That you despair
You still have a soul

Thank Your Maker
That you are smiling
You still have pleasure

Thank Your Maker
That you can see a physician
You are still alive

We Thank Our Maker
That you honor us with your presence
You are very welcome

# The Calming

What delights is the pleasure
The pleasure of seeking
I dare not taste your pleasures
For they are boundless

Where do you seek?
Ask the ocean
Moving and yet soothing
Cool and glistening
Keeps on going
But always at the same spot

Where do you search?
Ask the trees
They have peace
Stable and calm
They run with the wind
But always at the same spot

Oh what agony
I long to be the flower, beautiful, radiant,
Desired yet not consumed,
Loved passionately never heartbroken
Temporary, not forever, a short happy life
Till we appear at Your pleasure

# Guardians of Truth

They come in shades
Shades of Truth
Powerful, commanding, austere, and outwardly humble

The keepers of the Truth
They say they guard the Truth
They keep us straight

Till the madman says to them
"Careful there is a deep pit ahead!"
Then they stop, and then they look
They, the keepers of the Truth

# To the Love I Dared Oppose

I disagree with you sometimes
I condemn your deeds at others
I argue with you frequently
The rest of the time I oppose all your views

Yet I acknowledge your excellence
I admire the wisdom of your words
I celebrate the deeds that you do
Your footsteps I gladly celebrate

Yet out of love I disagree
To help you grow I challenge your words
Perfection of the mind leads to arrogance
I seek for you to bloom as your knowledge multiplies

For to challenge yourself is Socratic
To always question human action
Is to see endlessly
To be the best you need one hundred eyes

To see everything is not arrogance
Disagreement does not deny your essence
For even the prophets erred
And error breeds knowledge—or ignorance

To stay on top invite critique
To climb to the peak accept challenge
To win you need competition
To fly expect arrows

# Friendship

I am still your friend
Even though we walk different roads

I will always be your friend
Even though we rarely talk

I am your friend
Even when you don't see me

I remain your friend
Because you cannot buy another

We will remain friends
Even when I hurt you

For I was your friend
When you gave me love

I will be your friend
When the love simmers

I cherish you my friend
As we have memories too dear

I care for you my friend
Even in your darkest hour

I celebrate for you my friend
When you reach your peak

I desire you to stay my friend
Even when I never say it

I care for you my friend
And you have my heart wherever you are

I miss you my friend
When the dreams bring you

You will always be my friend
Even when you fall

Go well my friend
For our hearts shared a life that no pain can fleece

# My Fatherless Kids

Forgive me
My two best treasures
Are the loves of my life
They are my loves
My life, my desires
They indeed are the best of me

Please sir
Hear me
Speak me
Cry me
Believe me
They are my future

Judge me not
For you know me not
For it helps me not
And it helps you not
Allow me, condone me,
Understand me

My sins of yesterday
Are my loves of today
My inspirations for tomorrow
My dreams for the future
If you will let me be

For I have had a life
That you know not
A past that you desire not
A history that you wish not
So allow me to dream through these kids
That my pain may end

If you will let me
They will have a tomorrow
That I have not
Judge me not sir
For they are mine
For they are love

∽

# The Answer Inside You

Try hard to win
But do not try too hard
For if it seems impossible
You may be on the wrong track

Since surely tomorrow will come
An answer must exist to ease your way
For yesterday was and is now over
Yet the problem did not crush you

All the answers lay around us
But we do not ask for answers
Because we prefer to fight alone
As if asking is for losers

So in the vanity of knowing
We sweat the tears of labor
When asking could have cooled our tempo
Open eyes and a closed mind result in a blind heart

So go easy on yourself
Life was not meant to be tough
We live on earth not in hell
When it gets too hot as you try harder, ask

Do not sweat this life
Apathy may lead to distress
An honest day's work should feed your soul
If your efforts take you to hell maybe you are truly blind

෭

# Different Worlds, Same People

You come with freedom
Freedom of speech

I come with faith
And respect for all

You were born of enlightenment
And a vastly open mind

I have deep beliefs
And I walk according to the teachings

You decide your values
And believe in yourself

I am beholden to my Holy Book
And it is my map to life

You come with liberal values
And allow people to be

I come with gifts of my faith
For I am a testament of my religion

You allow all creeds to flourish
And all souls to shine

I am of the true teaching
And the way of heaven is my way

You are of a wealthy land
And you can create your heaven of bliss

I am of a deprived land
And my Holy Book is my contentment

You have access to all media
And information is free

I have mainly good news from the Book
And local gossip from the street corner

You live in a world where dreams come true
And anyone can fly

I am from a land where only heaven can save
And only the chosen could dare to dream

You who are free to think
See me only through your values

I whose thoughts are guided
See you through my values

So the free thinkers
And the deep followers of faith
Walk different paths
Yet reach the same conclusions
That tolerance is not a human virtue

# The Heart Wins

I got gold
Yet I desired sawdust

I got purity
Yet I wanted dirt

I got love
Yet I sought pain

I got peace
Yet I needed turmoil

I got joy
Yet I craved sorrow

I got roses
Yet I favored thorns

I got sheep
Yet I invited wolves

I got freedom
Yet I found bondage

I got wealth
Yet I bought penury

I got wisdom
Yet my heart always won

❧

# Funeral Day

I will be there
On your final day

I will be there
To wish you well

I will be there
In my nicest clothes

I will be there
In my diamonds

I will be there
With the rest of the crowd

I will be there
So I can be noticed

I will be there
To sing your praise

For I was not there
In your time of need

For I was missing
When you wanted comfort

For I was gone
When you needed warmth

For I was hiding
When you cried for help

For I was away
When you needed company

Yet today I am here
And everybody can see me

For the least I can do
Is to be pretty for you

❧

# Living Clean

If wealth were well spent
Then the water would flow

If we loved our land
The lights would shine

Life's safety net is not your fortune
But in the wealth of your land

Delight not in opulence
For you came to life naked

You may go forth with pretension
And try to buy tomorrow

But death will not be conquered
Your history cannot change

Live a beautiful story
So the heavens sing your name

Look at the limousine of life
To ride well all parts need to be in harmony

Allow the land to flourish
So when you fall there will be many soft spots

# Baton of Life

If you think I did good
Then recognize it

If I performed a good act
Do not thank me

If I did some good
Share it with someone else

For goodness is the baton of life
And the baton like life must keep going

So give the baton of goodness to the next winner
In turn the baton will get back to you with love

# My Door Is Shut

The door is shut
And the moon rules supreme

The door is closed
For out of darkness comes light

The door is locked
And dreams become actions

The door is shut
So you sing your wishes to the beloved

The door is closed
That protects your nectar

The door is locked
And the sweets of delight stay hidden

The door is shut
So your souls unite with love

The door is closed
And the purity stays golden

The door is locked
Venus is queen of the moment

My door is shut
And I conquered the sun

# Heaven Left Her Dreams

Every night she dreamt of heaven
Thus every night was joy
Because heaven appeared while she slept
And she knew she was with the Love

In her bliss she had peace
She glowed with faith and walked with grace
As each day she looked forward to the night
When Angels of love took her to heaven as she slept

Then Heaven walked away
Her dreams disappeared
She had enjoyed her heaven
But in her pleasure she had loved alone

Her dreams had become an opiate
She'd become intoxicated with the love
And did not share her visions
For the taste was so good she devoured it alone

The Creator gave freely
And gave her heaven with love
She failed to share the blessings
And now the fruits of Love were gone

In vain she walked the land
Looking for a savior to heal her loss
But no one had seen her dreams
The Love had not touched them

Now she strides the land in torment
Looking for her heaven
Among mortals she had forsaken
When she loved her Lord alone

So let her sorrow be your guide
When the Love has shown you grace
Remember to share your blessings
And let the world enjoy your dreams

❧

# Gifts

Too often we give people gifts, and we cannot let go. The true blessing of giving is in the wish or the desire to give. For giving should be free. Please give and resist the self-gratification of seeing the recipient use the gift. More important than the gift itself is the act of kindness.

True gifts are the gifts of love. Once, my dear, wonderful 70-year-old patient, who could barely walk with a fractured leg, forced herself into her car and drove halfway across the town to see me. She ambulated with a walker at the rate of one step every 5 minutes. It was a grueling journey. Her reason was because "her church magazine wanted doctors to advertise and she wanted to make sure I met the deadline."

This truly was a gift of a million years and was worth more than many physical material gifts I have ever received. We prefer to give material gifts rather than gifts of love.

Just call me and say "I love you" and forget the gloves. I cannot buy your love, but I can buy some gloves. So give me some priceless love. I will take a hug as well.

Sometimes, when I get a gift, I leave it in the plastic wrapping forever. For me to see it fresh and untouched reminds me of the love behind the gift. When I hear the question, "Did you not like my shirt?" I feel sad because the giver is taking back their love by demanding gratification. If I wear your gift, it does not mean I appreciate it. What I do with your gift may not reflect my heart. What is most important is your act of love.

For giving is done with finality. The best thank-you for a gift is in turn giving a gift to someone else who does not expect a gift. This gift could be some love, a warm smile, or an act of kindness. Try not to burden your soul by agonizing whether your gift was useful or not. If the recipient cannot see the kindness behind an unusable gift, then you both need to seek love. For the true gifts of life are love, friendship, loyalty, and kindness. And these are on sale at rock-bottom prices every day.

❧

# Lament of Africa

They came with God
They came with guns
They came with wine
So they could save us
And liberate us from darkness

For it was their religious duty
And their moral obligation
To civilize us
And to teach us their ways
For we were their burden

Previously we had lived in bliss
We did not ask to be saved
We did not know poverty
We lived united with nature
We never knew we were lost

But still they came
In the name of God
With missionaries and visionaries
Lush vegetations for industry
Rubber, palm oil, cotton, and timber galore

So we accepted God
And we loved him more passionately than our saviors
We had no substitute for God
And we learnt new cultures
And discarded our treasures for theirs

So we were saved
From our own selves
Where once we were not afraid
Now we feared each other
For where  we were humans now we were heathens

So we acquired new delights
And learnt the taste of refined sugar
Where once we preferred guava fruit
We now wanted chocolate
Yet before, the palm fruit held sway

79

Where we needed tomatoes
We got puree
And where mango was king
We desired the joys of wheat bread
As we claimed the cuisine of our saviors

We learnt the highs of whiskey
And the calming of teas
And the precision of left-handed eating
And the pleasure of tobacco
A new world, a new culture, a new master

For the savior had religion
For the winner had cannons
Maxim guns to quench dissent
And the conqueror was chosen
To rule us benevolently for our sake

Then off we went to war
Onward First World War
Forward Second World War
We died to block the fascists
From the tyranny of oppression

And then we woke up
Why die to liberate others
And come back home serfs?
We had tasted freedom
Freedom to die meant life was for the taking

So we asked the savior to leave
But we wanted his foods
And desired his life
We needed his science
As the seduction was complete

So now we had God
And we had learnt a new tongue
We now had public institutions
And where we were once nations
Now we were countries

For centuries we had lived off the land
Now TV said the city was the future
Within decades we abandoned the way of life
That had sustained us from time immemorial
And created city slums, misery, and despair

In the cities we learnt hunger and the power of money
We now discovered unemployment and massive crime
For cities do not grow food
And farming was a backward way to live
And cassava was now inferior to the hamburger

We now had freedom
And we were drunk with ability
A caged lion locked for centuries
Exalts in freedom but has no direction
For we were overflowing with the liquor of the victor

So in the maze of a new world
Countries were formed with no history
From baby to man
With no childhood or adolescence
A façade with no reality, a loss

In our loss
We tried to fly without wings
Civilizations are borne of history
But the history is your struggle
Not a dream that was carved out for you

Countries that have no soul
Are like ancient structures abandoned for centuries
Strong solid edifices outwardly
Impressive in appearance
With an earth-shattering absence of life

Oh what freedom awaits us
Where we were once people
Our new name was Independence
Now the master was gone
We had freedom to play with our fortunes

For when they left
We had our chance to prove them wrong
Yet we discovered strife
And we walked backwards
Yet we did not despair

In our attempt to be
We plundered our lands
And raped the treasures
And then worshipped God with all sincerity
And then gave back our souls to those who brought guns

We never fear because we have God
So as long as we worship
We can walk back centuries
For the desire to develop ourselves
Is not our greatest gift

So in vain we invented blame
Blame our rulers now
Blame our former masters
Blame everybody else
We who worship endlessly  of course blameless

When we bade the master goodbye
We still wanted his essence
Who wants to be saved from darkness
Just to experience a loss?
Maybe the master dropped his burden too soon

# I Think Therefore I Am Guilty

My heart is pure
My desire is golden
My dream is peace
My pleasure is giving

I have been blessed
I have been given wisdom
I have intellect
I have random thoughts

For my mind dares not think
For my duty is to obey man
For my creative expressions are taboo
For my outlook must be misery

Then I did not create myself
Then I did not seek a mind
Then I found myself with reason
Then I found my brain inquiring

Yet I have eyes that can see
Yet I have ears that can hear
Yet I have feet that can walk
Yet I have a mind that is banned

But I want no gold
But I pleasure only in thoughts
But I love my endless reasoning
But I am guilty when I think

That my faculties have a function
That my intellect was a mistake
That my enforcers are supreme
That my churning mind was an error

I am sure Who gave me brains
And Who gave me reason
And critical thinking
Expected me to use them

ᕦ

# A Common Enemy

A common enemy
Brings together unlikely partners
For nothing unites like a shared hate

Yes foes from days of yore
Today are best of friends
For together a greater evil must be crushed

Then who is the enemy
If he is today your friend
As you protect each other

Yet before you were ready to defeat him
And now that you have a bigger fear
You become best of friends

So then begs the question
Who is your enemy?
And who is the friend

Yesterday's enemy is today's friend
And today's friend will become the enemy
When the bigger enemies are gone

Then the enemy is truly you
For when you joined with a foe
You allowed hate to bond you

For when peace rules the waves
There was no need to bond
Since in the face of contentment the love of self wins

It is the art of survival
The ancient battle of the fittest
That friends can turn to foes

So the enemy of your enemy is your friend
While the friend of your enemy is your enemy
Life's choices dare to make reason but miss

So humans join together to fight a cause
But walk their separate ways when there is no cause to battle
For peace divides and war unites

# Vermin Daddy

You were meant to be my father
Yet you slew my soul
Drank of my innocence
And drained me of tears

You were chosen to be my guide
Yet you blinded my vision
Ate of my heart
And chewed on my emotions

You were appointed as my protector
Yet you terrorized my life
Devoured all my pleasure
And banished me to shame

You should have been a comfort
Yet you bathed me in evil
Deprived me of happiness
And ended my sleep

You were revered on the outside
Yet my mother you terrorized
The public you charmed
And the world you deceived

Well today I can smile
For you have left this world
For I have made this journey regardless
For the Lord held my hand

You could not destroy my faith
You could not break my heart
I will be the eagle
While you remain the remorseless vulture

I have cast you out of my being
For I have this one life
And your predation did not destroy me
For you sold your soul for fire

As I throw you away with the rubbish
I pray that your soul is penitent
For I know all my prayers
Will not free your fate from hell

# The Right to Ask

How do you ask
By expressing your needs

How do you receive
By giving thanks

To desire
You must first sacrifice

The best gifts go to those
Who give love freely

When you give love for free
The privilege to ask is payback for love

# Why Am I Lonely?

Because you live alone
47 years old
No children
No spouse
Nobody but you

You like to live clean
And avoid the nightlife
The intoxicants and the gambling
You crave human company
Yet none is forthcoming

So every evening after work
You shut yourself up at home
To devour ice cream and chips
And spend quality time with Mr. TV
Then you swim the River Self-Pity to bed

You feel cheated that you are alone
That you have nobody
Yet tonight as you walked into your home
You waved hello to your neighbor
That neighbor who lives alone, confined to a wheelchair

This lonely crippled neighbor
What did she do when she could walk?
Did she wave goodbye to other cripples?
Or did she give love?
Only her soul can tell

In your loneliness, spare a thought for your neighbor
You do not spend your evenings with her
Maybe if you share your sunshine
The brightness you give will open back doors of love
To demand love, you must first give love

# What Is a Friend

A good friend
Exalts in your achievements
Protects your name
Sings your praises
Dries your tears
And walks with you

An unsafe friend
Avoids you when you are ill
Hides when you are helpless
Laughs when you fall
Despises you when you need help
And wants to better you

A true friend
Tells you the truth
Does not envy your success
Wants you to have more regardless
Is there with you always
Will pray for your happiness

An avoidable friend
Needs something from you
Runs away when you cry
Listens to your miseries to mock you
Offers you selfish advice
Only wants your fortune

A better friend
Can be reliable
Will be supportive
May love you in your hour of shame
Does not judge your failings
But will show you the right way

Too often we pick only friends who are convenient
And drop friends who are unable to help us today
Forgetting days past when they proved themselves
When you are down you will know your true friends
Remember you selfishly picked the absent ones
Because once upon a time they were convenient for you

# Love and Desire

You do not have to own
The object of your love

Desire is not love
Love is not ownership

Love those you do not desire
Like you desire those you do not love

Things we love may hurt us
What we love is not always right for us

Desire makes us wade in lust and greed
The pursuit of forbidden desires is not love

How do you consume what you love
If what you truly love should be preserved

True love is fulfillment without possession
A satiety that no desire can drown

# I Have a Baby Daddy

Yes I have a baby daddy
He ain't got no job

Yes I have me a man
Who drives my ride

My baby daddy hangs
As I work two jobs

Yeah my baby daddy
Someday he gonna rap

I will have his babies
Buy his clothes
Pay his traffic tickets
Buy him some dope
And take him to the mall
For I work hard
So my man can bring me lunch

# My Soul Can Hurt No One

Life is acceptance
So accept the best
And expect the worst
For goodness may not bring joy today
While evil may bring instant pleasure

Even if you sincerely repent
And walk a path of thorns
You may not find the way
For when you try to seek
The load of knowing weighs

As you strive to stay on the path
You do not always please
For the human soul is weak
So the crooked road is used
And the feet that walk straight are feared

So where do you walk?
Since the world expects weakness
And to be virtuous is unreal,
The burden of goodness is love
To love you last is the way

Yet we blind ourselves to truth
And we live a life of deceit
Though we speak in tongues of the blessed
Yet our hearts live in our feet
And our souls we have left for yonder

So if you want peace
Accept it in your soul
For another cannot give it
And humans expect pretense
And your purity is suspicious

So then walk your way
And try not to be the hypocrite
Let your heart glow with Love
And do not hurt another
That was created by love

∽

94

# Thank You Is Not Music

So you like the words "thank you"
Then thank the one who gave you life
Before you demand thanks

Who gave you life gave you a mind
But your mind strayed from Love
Yet you now feel you deserve thanks

Giving is the drum of life
Kindness is the chant of Prophets
Love is the orchestra of heaven

Till you lose your mind thanking the Love
Till you give without being seen
Till you stop your self-adoration

"Thank you" will always be your burden
The lullaby of love is not "thank you"
The song of your heart needs no words

# Child of Athens

My name is Mr. Democracy
I come here to defend my nature
For many actions are performed in my name
Many acts good and wonderful
Others strange and desperate

I was born in Greece in the fifth century B. C.
My parents were Athenian males
No woman was involved in my creation
A child procreated only by males
Is the reason for my convoluted nature

From the beginning it was difficult to be me
Was I the preserve of rich landowners
Or could I be used by lesser serfs?
If I was to champion equality,
How could I escape being a weapon of the poor

Traditional societies need the wealthy for commerce
And the poor to pay taxes and bear the burdens
This was not my making
Yet I, Democracy, was asked to intervene
I, borne with no feminine touch to heal men's divisiveness

The confusion of my birth was deep
The poor could tyrannize landowners with votes
But even Socrates himself
Underestimated the power of wealth
To control the votes of the poor

Adam Smith worried about me too
Even the impoverished forgot the poor
Everybody wanted me to protect the wealthy
After all the winner takes it all
And I was not born to champion the dispossessed

So I remain a tool
Termed the basis of good governance
Yet many despots and tyrants use me
And the world seems to be in denial
Power always rest in the hands of oligarchs

I have been reinvented to justify power
For rarely in my life has a commoner achieved
To succeed in my name is not about being the best
To succeed in me it pays to be part of the status quo
The oligarchy of wealth, birth, religion, or education

People still try to define me
They vote for their leaders
Yet the leaders become independent of the voters
Once voted in they do not need your votes to act
I am freedom to vote for others who will think for you

So I am Mr. Democracy
Some of the best rulers were not democrats
And some of the worst tyrants were voted in
I am just a tool
Many wars fought in my imperfect name

I have not always been a glorious name
I have presided over slavery
ruled over genocides
justified corruption
facilitated majority oppression

Yet in my other life
I have stimulated freedoms
Championed liberties
Enabled individual success
And allowed freedom of speech

At my time of conception I was accountable
I could easily be questioned by anyone
I could be voted by all but women and the poor
Now things are reversed
The rulers are not accountable but the poor and women can vote

Too often I am confused with freedom to vote
I am also freedom to question
As well as freedom to receive criticism
Freedom to respect the rule of law
And freedom of information

I am Democracy
Daughter of freedom
Cousin of free speech
Sister of liberty
Mother of accountability

I have a complex history
Once I get in the motion
I always overcome
Does not make me perfect
Except in the hands of great mortals

I am the scourge of kings
Nemesis of communism
The willing tool of tyrants
Revolutionaries confuse me with freedom
Idealists need me to champion change

The mighty empires caved in to me
The British through the Magna Carta
USA with the constitution
The Greeks, Ottomans, Mayans, the Fulani
I am knocking at the doors of Arabia, China, and Russia

Call me Democracy
All religions need me
I—conceived by pagans
For I am the will of the people
My imperfections still give change a chance

So sing my name
Scream with joy
I am here to uplift you
No one can stop me
It is I, Democracy, son of Athens

# But Once

It takes but one love to define your life

It takes but one try to conquer your fears

It takes but one dream to achieve your goals

It takes but one chance to make your move

It takes but one life to prove yourself

# From Mars to Africa with Love

I came from Mars to visit planet Earth
Along the way I stopped on Jupiter to see my friends
I had to announce to the Universe
I was going learn about human beings

I landed in Europe with all its beauty
And sojourned in America the land of gold
And took a lovely cruise to Asia
Finally to the Swiss where all the money was

The banks of the Swiss were full of dollars
These dollars just resting in peace
"But why this free money"? I asked
"The Africans" was their reply

I was touched and really impressed
Who were these kind people called the Africans?
For surely they must be the kings of Earth
To give the Swiss all this money to play with

I flew to Africa in full throttle to learn from the best
And I landed in the airport with no electricity
I drove into the city and I saw misery
I turned around and hunger was everywhere

I went farther inland and saw disease
Running water was a luxury
Yet everybody had two cell phones
I asked the Africans "What say you?"

They looked at me the green Martian
All they wanted was a seat on my space ship
"Not this time" I said "for in Mars we like ourselves"
"We keep our fortunes to develop Mars only"

I asked the King of Africa
Why all the money in the Alps?
"What about water, light, good hospitals, and food?"
"My home in London has all that" was his reply

I fled to Mars never to return
"Africans are strange" was my report
For never in the solar system were there a people
Who gave away their souls on a platter of gold

# The Master

To seek knowledge
To desire truth

That which falls from a fountain
That which sprays forth wisdom

The student of truth
Has lived a life of knowledge

Piety and abstinence
Are vital parts of wisdom

To deliver the truth
A master has sacrificed desire

The ability to be selfless
Is to be content with the present

To justify your failings
Is to feed your passions

The truly wise man
Does not need to explain his deeds

A true master lives his actions
Every act a story of moral courage

# Gifts Galore

An empty farm, long forgotten
You found an old sack
Filled with gold
A gift from God or someone else's wealth

A beautiful house
Belonging to a debtor now bankrupt
Sold to you for pennies on the dollar
A gift from God or someone else's loss

Who decides what is best?
For only the future will tell
Since your loss may be a blessing
Just as your gain may be a curse

So if unexpected treasures come your way
Treat them with humility or
Return them to their rightful owners
For the Lord tests us with Gifts Galore

# Ultimate Wine

I am Ultimate Wine
Call me devil juice
I pollute minds
And corrupt nations
Yet I am irresistible

I am black oil
The most beautiful black fluid of all
I glisten in the sun
As I shine with wealth
Taste me once and you are hooked

Oh joy, oh comfort
Grown men cry when I spring forth
Countries convulse as I flow steady
The world bows to me
I am the kingmaker of Earth

Nobody stands in my way
Instead they refine me
So I can lubricate their wealth
What a joy it is to be me
The spoiler of mankind

Many names describe me
Some call me crude
Others call me black gold
Only I can swing from crude to gold
And still be desired by all regardless

Industries need me to function
Armies cannot move without me
My products are used for cooking
And roads are built from my fractions
You need me to see at night

No opium or hashish can touch my pleasure
I corrupt the most holy
I intoxicate the most learned
I am responsible for more destruction
Than any addictive substance

I am truly trouble
Not all countries can handle me
Because I steal their souls
And seduce their morals
For I am the nectar of the devil

Many wars are fought on my behalf
Local industries crushed in my name
Ecologies destroyed as humans crave my soul
I am the miracle of overnight wealth
The ultimate wine that intoxicates mankind

# Friendly Souls

It may be wiser to dine with snakes
Sleep with vultures, consort with hawks
And sleep on a bed of thorns
Than to walk with those who feed off your soul,
Bathe with your sweat and devour your goodness

When you sleep on a beautiful bed of roses
You may fail to see the pointed daggers beneath
Honey, the essence of sweetness and the great cure,
Is created by bees with killer stings
Pleasure and pain are strange twins

# It Was Your Cousin

I am angry
I am sad
I am agitated
Where art thou, daddy?

Daddy, Daddy
Where art thou?
I cannot see you
And I miss you

You are locked up
Somewhere in a strange place
I cannot reach you
I miss your tender touch

They say it was not you
It was really your cousin
And you went in for him
Because your cousin was a rat

I want to be proud of you
I want to see your strong muscles
I want to hear your booming voice
I need you to protect me

Promise me you will be home soon
And you will stay home every night
Not with your cousins and unknown aunties
Stay with me and be my father

# You Are Nothing

You came from nothing
You are nothing
You are afraid to be nothing
You will be nothing
Be absent from yourself and you will feel nothing

# Ignorance Is Knowledge

The most knowledgeable amongst us
Are driven by the fuel of their own ignorance

# Unshakeable Faith

Show me a person
Trapped in a fire
Checking the religious belief
Of his rescuer
And I will show you
Unshakeable faith

# Can You Forgive?

I dare not forgive you
Because it is not my privilege
The honor to forgive you
Comes from the Creator

The Lord who made you
Sees your own heart
And in His mercy let you be
For you did not wrong Him

I thought you had wronged me
Yet you had no desire to harm me
In my myopic view I judged you
While your Maker still gives you favor

Despite my feelings
Your creator did not forsake you
And you have continued to prosper
For you are loved by the Beloved

He who created you
Desires not my advice on those He favors
So I am not in a position to forgive
I should seek pardon myself

# Listen to the Rain Drops

Listen my friend
Listen to the rain drops
Listen to the winds

Hear my friend
Hear the voices
Hear the sounds

Understand my friend
Understand the message
Understand the sentiments

Look my friend
Look at your blessings
Look at your growth

Watch my friend
Watch your covered pudding
Watch your front gates

Think my friend
Think like the enemy
Think how you could be destroyed

Reflect my friend
Reflect on the mistakes of the fallen
Reflect on your actions

Act my friend
Act with the cunning of the hyena
Act under the cover of darkness

Shield my friend
Shield your weapon
Shield your strength from the enemy

Show, my friend
Show your innocent side
Show the world what it wants to see

Avoid my friend
Avoid chasing the storm clouds
Avoid searching for single carpenter ants

Build my friend
Build a fortress to withstand the elements
Build for prevention not for correction

Win my friend
Win the race with stealth
Win easy without dust

# King of the Hill

I am not of the mouse
I am but a king
A lion A warrior
The Lord of the hills

The fearless shark
The bravest of heroes
The majestic camel
I am never of the rat

Trepidation surrounds my shadow
For I am the sun and the darkness
The stallion and the tiger
Never did weakness know my nature

I am the falcon swift as light
The volcano spewing energy
The rainstorm that respects no one
No fear shall touch my soul

I am the tornado faster than lightning
My family is my passion
I am the bull protecting the pack
Not the doe that hides

I am the king of today
The earthquake that has no master
So let my thunderous voice and crushing footsteps
Show that I am not of the forgotten

# The Thief Of This Life

Give, give, give
Do not walk like
The world owes you

After all you breathe air
Walk on the earth
And eat of it's fruits

Using nostrils you did not create
Limbs you did not build
And a digestive system you did not invent

And yet you continue to take
That which is not yours
With tools you did not create

You cannot survive in isolation
All life needs the interactions of nature to exist
The trees, flowers, birds and rocks affect your life

Yet you live only for yourself
Demanding more each day
Forgetting the balance of forces

You take but do not give back
And when your soul is in turmoil
You look again to outside forces to heal you

The vicious cycle is you
You stole of nature
Never giving never sharing

Nature is continuously exchanging
Add to the cycle by sharing your gifts
And the blessings of nature will find you

So, do not be the thief of this life
Start by giving, giving, giving
And the world will give you back handsomely

❧

# About the Author

Zakari Tata holds an Adjunct Clinical Professorship position in Family Medicine at Wayne State University in Detroit, as well as Michigan State University in Lansing. He trained as a General Surgeon in England and is a Fellow of the Royal College in Ireland. Dr. Tata is a Bioethist, a staunch advocate of humanitarian medicine, and has a strong interest in philosophy and writing. Based on his life experiences with people from all walks of life and his travels around the world, he has produced inspirational and philosophical poetry that has a universal appeal. He is active in community working with youths and the underprivileged. He has also given presentations on Bioethics at the American Society of Bioethics and Humanities.